smoothies
AND JUICES

A selection of refreshing and invigorating drinks

Christine Ambridge & Sarah Beattie

BARNES
& NOBLE
NEW YORK

© 2004 by Parragon Books Ltd.

This 2006 edition published by Barnes & Noble Publishing, Inc.
by arrangement with Parragon Publishing.

Produced by
THE BRIDGEWATER BOOK COMPANY

2006 Barnes & Noble Publishing

ISBN-13 : 978-0-7607-8480-8
ISBN-10 : 0-7607-8480-9

Printed and bound in China
1 3 5 7 9 10 8 6 4 2

Notes for the reader

o This book uses both imperial, metric, or US cup measurements. Follow the same
units of measurement throughout; do not mix imperial and metric.

o All spoon measurements are level: teaspoons are assumed to be 5 ml, and
tablespoons are assumed to be 15 ml.

o Unless otherwise stated, milk is assumed to be whole, eggs and individual
vegetables such as carrots are medium, and pepper is freshly ground black pepper.

o Recipes using raw eggs should be avoided by infants, the elderly, pregnant women,
convalescents, and anyone suffering from an illness.

contents

There is such an array of exotic fruits available today, and blending them into a delicious smoothie or using them for innovative juices is an excellent way to enjoy them all year round.

introduction

We are all more health-conscious than we used to be, and are more informed about artificial additives, sugar, sweeteners, and preservatives in our food. Some commercial drinks may look healthy enough, but a closer look at the label will reveal that they contain a number of chemicals we would rather do without. These drinks can be rather too sweet, or bland and unappetizing. It makes sense, therefore, to blend your own fruit and vegetable drinks. This way, you can be sure that what you are drinking contains no hidden additives and you can also opt for organic raw ingredients. Once you get into the habit of making your own drinks, you will find yourself buying commercial varieties less and less.

We are encouraged to eat about five portions of fresh fruit and vegetables a day, but our modern hectic lifestyles means this is often impossible. Consuming them in drink form is a quick, easy, and agreeable way to ensure we keep to this target and receive the recommended daily amount of vitamins we need. You can devise your own smoothie and juice recipes, based on your favorite ingredients, but the rule is that it is usually best not to combine fruit and vegetables in any one drink. Exceptions to this rule are apples, carrots, and tomatoes, which blend happily with most other ingredients.

If you are going to be creating your own drinks recipes on a regular basis, it makes sense to keep a well-stocked fruit bowl at all times, with apples, oranges, grapes, and other fruit. Do not be afraid to experiment with fruit that may be unfamiliar to you, such as pomegranates, watermelon, or guavas, as they make delicious and refreshingly palate-cleansing drinks. You will also find it a good idea to keep a generous supply of frozen fruit in the freezer at all times, such as bananas, strawberries, blackberries, and peaches. Use them straight from the freezer to make a refreshing, chilled drink at any time of the year.

Whenever you have a surplus of fruit, freeze some away for future use in drinks and then you can enjoy your favorite fruit even when it is out of season. Freeze banana slices in a single layer on a tray, then transfer them to freezer bags. You can do the same with small chunks or slices of other fruits. Combined with your favorite ice cream or sherbet, they can be turned into mouth watering drinks at the drop of a hat. Keep lots of ice cubes in the freezer, too, and a plentiful supply of mineral water, milk, and yogurt in the refrigerator.

You do not need a wide range of fancy or expensive equipment to make your own drinks. Some basic utensils will do the job perfectly well. For the best results, use a food processor and a juicer.

equipment

A standard food processor can produce a smoothie in a matter of seconds with no trouble at all. If you do not have a food processor, you can use a blender for many of the recipes, but it should be a fairly resilient model.

Unlike a food processor, which turns ingredients into a purée, a juicer separates the juice from the pulp of a fruit. Juicers vary in price and performance and range from the more inexpensive centrifugal ones, which extract the juice by means of centrifugal force, to the more expensive hydraulic varieties, which may seem an extravagance but produce really excellent results by retaining plenty of nutrients. Triturating juicers are in the middle of both the price and nutritional range. The hydraulic type is best because the juice is forced out through extreme pressure, retaining all the essential nutrients, and so, if you are a great natural juice fan, this is the obvious choice for you.

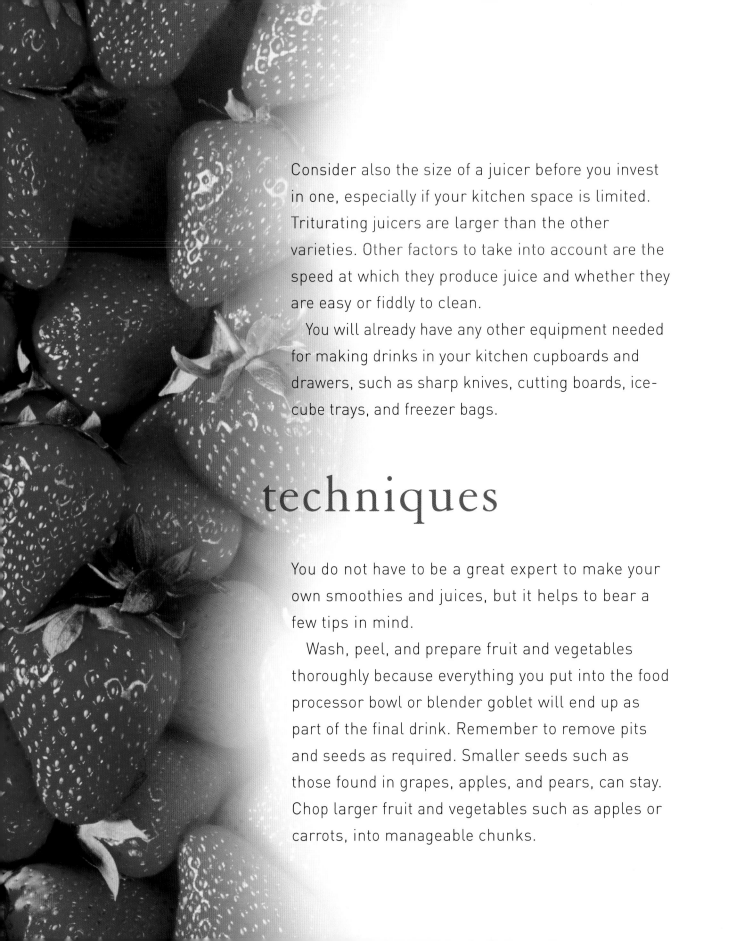

Consider also the size of a juicer before you invest in one, especially if your kitchen space is limited. Triturating juicers are larger than the other varieties. Other factors to take into account are the speed at which they produce juice and whether they are easy or fiddly to clean.

You will already have any other equipment needed for making drinks in your kitchen cupboards and drawers, such as sharp knives, cutting boards, ice-cube trays, and freezer bags.

techniques

You do not have to be a great expert to make your own smoothies and juices, but it helps to bear a few tips in mind.

Wash, peel, and prepare fruit and vegetables thoroughly because everything you put into the food processor bowl or blender goblet will end up as part of the final drink. Remember to remove pits and seeds as required. Smaller seeds such as those found in grapes, apples, and pears, can stay. Chop larger fruit and vegetables such as apples or carrots, into manageable chunks.

Crush ice cubes before you add them to the food processor, or you will damage the sharp blade. To do this, place them between two clean dish towels and hammer them with a rolling pin.

With juicers, you do not need to peel most fruit and vegetables, except for tough-skinned varieties such as bananas, kiwifruit, and citrus fruit, but you should always wash them thoroughly first. More heavy-duty juicers can cope with tough skins, such as melon skin, but check the manufacturer's directions carefully before taking a risk. Many of the essential nutrients in fruit and vegetables are found just close to the skin, so it can be important to retain it during juicing for maximum health benefits. Always remember to use fresh and unblemished fruit and vegetables.

Enjoy making up your own drinks recipes, whether a juice, smoothie, slush, float, or milk shake. Be bold and imaginative in your flavor and color combinations. Devising your own drinks is healthy, easy, and, above all, great fun.

smoothies

are a delicious way to enjoy fruit all year round. Whenever you have a surplus of fruit, don't just reach for jelly recipes. Instead, why not set some aside for drinks? Simply prepare and freeze them in the usual way, and you will have a constant supply of frozen fruit ready to use for drinks at any time of the year. This is an ideal way to enjoy fruits, even when they are out of season.

mango &
orange smoothie

If you want
a *creamy smoothie,*

use **vanilla ice cream** instead of mango sherbet. The **mango** must be quite ripe and fragrant. It should be soft and yield to **gentle pressure**.

SERVES 2

1 large ripe mango

juice of 2 medium oranges

3 scoops of mango sherbet

DECORATION

1 strip of orange zest

Place the mango on a cutting board and cut lengthwise through the flesh as close to the large flat central pit as possible. Turn it over and do the same thing on the other side of the pit. Remove the peel and coarsely chop the flesh before placing in a processor.

Add the orange juice and sherbet and process until smooth.

Serve at once, decorated with a strip of orange zest if liked.

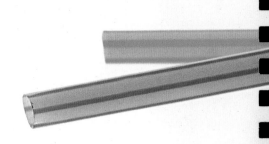

This drink combines the *rich flavors*

and **colors of summer fruits** in one superb smoothie.

Pour the orange juice into a food processor. Add the banana and half of the forest fruits and process until smooth.

Add the remaining forest fruits and process until smooth. Pour the mixture into tall glasses and decorate the rims with slices of fresh strawberry.

Add straws and serve.

SERVES 2

1$\frac{1}{2}$ **cups orange juice**

1 banana, sliced and frozen

3 cups frozen forest fruits (such as blueberries, raspberries, and blackberries)

DECORATION

slices of fresh strawberry

forest
fruit smoothie

pear,
orange,
& ginger reviver

Pretty
and *fragrant*,

with the **warmth of ginger**,
this smoothie will **brighten**
a less than perfect **summer's day**.

SERVES 2

**2 large ripe Bartlett
or similar juicy pears**

juice of 4 medium oranges

4 cubes candied ginger

Peel the pears and cut into fourths, removing the cores. Put into a food processor with the orange juice and the candied ginger and process until smooth.

Pour into glasses and serve.

The very *brief* cooking of *the fruits*

just **mellows the flavors** and lets the colors from the **damsons** and **plums** seep into the **apples** and **pears**.

SERVES 2

Put the pear, apple, plums, damson plums, and water into a small pan. Cover tightly, then set over medium heat and bring slowly to a boil. Take off the heat and let cool. Chill.

Put the fruit and water into a food processor and process until smooth.

Pour into glasses and serve.

1 ripe pear, peeled and cut into fourths

1 apple, peeled and cut into fourths

2 large red or dark plums, halved and pitted

4 ripe damson plums, halved and pitted

generous $^3/_4$ cup water

orchard
fruit
smoothie

blueberry
dazzler

Sweet, sharp, fragrant, *rich,* and *creamy*—

this is pure **magic** in a glass.

SERVES 2

³/₄ **cup apple juice**

¹/₂ **cup plain yogurt**

1 banana, sliced and frozen

generous 1 cup frozen blueberries

DECORATION

whole fresh blueberries

Pour the apple juice into a food processor. Add the yogurt and process until smooth.

Add the banana and half of the blueberries and process well, then add the remaining blueberries and process until smooth.

Pour the mixture into tall glasses and add straws.

Decorate with whole fresh blueberries and serve.

Use *Champagne* or *Muscat* grapes

to add to the **delicate floweriness** of this **light smoothie**.

Put the grapes, mineral water, frozen yogurt, and elderflower cordial in a food processor and process until smooth.

Pour into glasses and serve immediately.

SERVES 2

generous $1/2$ cup white grapes, deseeded or seedless

generous $3/4$ cup sparkling mineral water

2 large scoops of frozen yogurt (plain)

$1 1/2$ tbsp elderflower cordial

white grape

elderflower foam

blueberry
thrill

Blueberries are still a *much underrated* pleasure.

In this smoothie their **raw, tart sweetness** is **enhanced** by the yogurt.

SERVES 2

scant ½ cup strained plain yogurt

scant ½ cup water

scant 1 cup frozen blueberries

DECORATION

whole frozen blueberries

Put the yogurt, water, and blueberries into a food processor and process until smooth.

Pour into glasses and top with whole frozen blueberries.

An *invigorating* and *creamy smoothie*

to **lift your mood** and remind you of **tropical beaches.**

Pour the pineapple juice and coconut milk into a food processor. Add the ice cream and process until smooth.

Add the pineapple chunks and process until smooth.

Pour the mixture into scooped-out coconut shells, or tall glasses, and decorate with grated fresh coconut.

Add straws and serve.

1¹/₂ cups pineapple juice

¹/₃ cup coconut milk

5¹/₂ oz/150 g vanilla ice cream

1 cup frozen pineapple chunks

DECORATION

2 tbsp grated fresh coconut

TO SERVE

2 scooped-out coconut shells, optional

coconut
cream

strawberry
surprise

This *supremely* thirst-quenching *smoothie*

is ideal to serve on **scorching summer days**. The balsamic vinegar brings out the flavor of the **strawberries** beautifully.

SERVES 2

scant 1 cup frozen strawberries

generous ¾ cup ice-cold water

1 tbsp balsamic vinegar

1 tbsp flowery clear honey, such as acacia

Put the strawberries, water, balsamic vinegar, and honey in a food processor and process until smooth.

Pour into glasses and serve decorated with the mint.

DECORATION

fresh mint sprigs

Use the *bottling* liquid

as well as the fruit for this sharp, **thirst-quenching** smoothie.

Put the cherries with their bottling liquid into a food processor with the yogurt, then process until smooth.

Taste and sweeten with sugar if necessary.

Pour into glasses and serve with almond cookies.

SERVES 2

9 oz/250 g bottled morello cherries

$^2/_3$ cup strained plain yogurt

sugar, to taste

TO SERVE

almond cookies

DECORATION

cherries on a toothpick

cherry

sour

melon
refresher

Incorporating *three* different *types of melons,*

the flavor of this smoothie is both **delicate** and **refreshing** on a hot day.

SERVES 2

1 cup plain yogurt

3¹/₂ oz/100 g galia melon, cut into chunks

3¹/₂ oz/100 g cantaloupe melon, cut into chunks

3¹/₂ oz/100 g watermelon, cut into chunks

6 ice cubes, crushed

DECORATION

wedges of melon

Pour the yogurt into a food processor. Add the galia melon chunks and process until smooth.

Add the cantaloupe and watermelon chunks along with the ice cubes and process until smooth.

Pour the mixture into glasses and decorate with wedges of melon.

Serve at once.

Too *good*
just for Tuesdays,

this is **Ruby Anyday**.

SERVES 2

Cut the grapefruit into fourths, then pull off the peel and as much pith as possible. Discard any seeds.

Put the grapefruit and water into a food processor and process until smooth. Add the yogurt and honey and process again until combined.

Pour into glasses and serve at once.

1 large ripe pink or ruby grapefruit

scant $\frac{1}{2}$ cup ice-cold water

scant $\frac{1}{2}$ cup strained plain yogurt

1 tbsp flowery clear honey, such as acacia

ruby

anyday

gooseberry
foolish

It is *foolish* indeed to *ignore* gooseberries.

Ripe and fragrant, they have a rich fruitiness that combines **brilliantly** with custard-style yogurt. Dessert gooseberries are not small and green but large and a deep **plummy red**.

SERVES 2

1²/₃ **cup ripe dessert gooseberries**
generous ³/₄ cup water
2–4 tbsp golden granulated sugar
generous ³/₄ cup custard-style vanilla yogurt

DECORATION
a few slivered almonds

Put the gooseberries, water, and sugar into a small pan. Cover tightly, then place over medium heat and simmer for about 15 minutes, or until the gooseberries have split and are very soft. Let cool.

Put the gooseberries and their cooking liquid into a food processor and process until smooth. Add the yogurt and process again until combined.

Pour into glasses and sprinkle with slivered almonds to serve.

This long,
cool, *thirst-quencher*

will **revitalize** you when you are feeling **tired or stressed**.

Pour the pineapple juice, lemon juice, and water into a food processor. Add the sugar and yogurt and process until blended.

Add the peach and pineapple chunks and process until smooth.

Pour the mixture into glasses and decorate the rims with wedges of fresh pineapple.

Serve at once.

SERVES 2

$1/2$ cup pineapple juice

juice of 1 lemon

scant $1/2$ cup water

3 tbsp brown sugar

generous $3/4$ cup plain yogurt

1 peach, cut into chunks and frozen

$3/4$ cup frozen pineapple chunks

DECORATION

wedges of fresh pineapple

pineapple
tango

papaya
*sweet
& sour*

Papaya *undergoes* an amazing *transformation as it ripens.*

With the outside skin yellow, the **soft ripe papaya** is a **deep sunset pink** inside. Unripe, the dark green rind can be peeled away to reveal the **crisp light green**, tart fruit with a texture similar to that of an apple.

SERVES 2

9 oz/250 g ripe soft papaya
$^3/_4$ cup ice-cold water
juice of 1 lime

DECORATION
slices of green papaya

Peel the ripe papaya, discarding any seeds. Cut into chunks.

Put the papaya chunks into a food processor with the water and lime and process until smooth.

Pour into glasses and decorate with slices of green papaya.

Pink,
light, and *fruity*,

this **refreshing smoothie** is simply delicious. If you don't like the seeds, you can use a strainer to make it **silken smooth**.

SERVES 2

Peel the pears and cut into fourths, removing the cores. Put into a food processor with the raspberries and water and process until smooth.

Taste and sweeten with honey if the raspberries are a little sharp.

Pour into glasses and serve.

2 large ripe Anjou pears

scant 1 cup frozen raspberries

generous ¾ cup ice-cold water

honey, to taste

DECORATION

raspberries on a toothpick

pear &
raspberry delight

spiced
apple smoothie

Apple and *banana*

blended with spices

makes this a **sophisticated choice** of smoothie.

SERVES 2

1 cup apple juice

$\frac{1}{2}$ tsp powdered cinnamon

2 tsp grated fresh gingerroot

2 bananas, sliced and frozen

DECORATION

slices of fresh banana on a toothpick

Pour the apple juice into a food processor. Add the cinnamon and ginger and process gently until combined.

Add the banana and process until smooth.

Pour the mixture into tall glasses and decorate with slices of fresh banana on toothpicks.

Serve immediately.

Use a *strawberry* *ice cream* to contrast

with the **glorious green** color of this smoothie, or a **lime sherbet** to tone in with it. Whichever you choose, **the combination** will be delightful.

SERVES 2

Put the kiwifruit and lemonade into a food processor and process until smooth.

Pour into glasses and top with a scoop of ice cream or sherbet.

Serve at once.

4 ripe kiwifruit,
peeled and cut into fourths

generous ¾ cup traditional sparkling lemonade

2 large scoops of ice cream or sherbet

kiwi
cooler

apricot &
orange smoothie

This *smoothie* makes a great

vitamin-and mineral-packed breakfast in a glass.

SERVES 2

1 cup boiling water

scant 1 cup dried apricots

juice of 4 medium oranges

2 tbsp plain yogurt

1 tsp soft dark brown sugar

Put the apricots in a bowl and pour the boiling water over them. Let soak overnight.

In the morning, put the apricots and their soaking water into a food processor and process until puréed. Add the orange juice to the apricots in the food processor, and process until combined.

Pour into glasses and top with 1 tablespoon of yogurt and a sprinkling of brown sugar.

The *haunting* flavor of *green tea*

combines brilliantly with **golden-yellow plums**. If the weather isn't wonderful, this smoothie is just as delicious **served warm**.

SERVES 2

1 green tea with Eastern spice tea bag

1¹⁄₄ cups boiling water

1 tbsp sugar

²⁄₃ cup ripe yellow plums, halved and pitted

Put the tea bag in a teapot or pitcher and pour over the boiling water. Let infuse for 7 minutes. Remove and discard the tea bag. Let chill.

Pour the chilled tea into a food processor. Add the sugar and plums and process until smooth.

Serve at once.

green tea &
yellow plum
smoothie

breakfast

smoothie

Kick-start
your day

with this rich vitamin- and mineral-packed energizer.

SERVES 2

1 cup orange juice
½ cup plain yogurt
2 eggs
2 bananas, sliced and frozen

Pour the orange juice and yogurt into a food processor and process gently until combined.

Add the eggs and frozen bananas and process until smooth.

DECORATION
slice of fresh banana

Pour the mixture into glasses and decorate the rims with a slice of fresh banana.

Add straws and serve.

Note: this recipe contains raw eggs, so should be avoided by infants, the elderly, pregnant women, convalescents, and anyone suffering from an illness.

A *great favorite* in *Greece*,

where **roadside stalls** sell enormous watermelons, this smoothie makes the most of this gigantic fruit's **juiciness**.

SERVES **2**

1 wedge of watermelon, weighing about 12 oz/350 g

ice cubes

DECORATION

fresh mint sprigs

Cut the rind off the watermelon. Chop the watermelon into chunks, discarding any seeds.

Put the watermelon chunks into a food processor and process until smooth.

Place ice cubes in the glasses. Pour the watermelon mixture over the ice and serve decorated with the mint.

watermelon
refresher

elderflower
& pear smoothie

Make this
smoothie

in **late spring** or **early summer** when the elder bushes are in **full bloom**.

SERVES 2

4 small firm pears

2 heads of elder flowers,
freshly picked (or a dash of cordial)

1 strip of lemon zest

1 tbsp soft brown sugar

4 tbsp water

generous ¾ cup lowfat milk

TO SERVE

cats' tongues

Peel the pears and cut into fourths, discarding the cores. Place in a pan with the elder flowers, a strip of lemon zest, the sugar, and water. Cover tightly and simmer until the pears are very soft. Let cool.

Discard the elder flowers and lemon zest. Put the pears, cooking liquid, and milk into a food processor and process until smooth.

Serve immediately with cats' tongues.

The impeccable combination of *fresh flavors*

makes this one of the **most popular** smoothies.

SERVES 2

½ **cup plain yogurt**

¾ **cup strawberry yogurt**

¾ **cup orange juice**

scant 1¼ cups frozen strawberries

1 banana, sliced and frozen

DECORATION

slice of orange

whole fresh strawberry

Pour the plain and strawberry yogurts into a food processor and process gently. Add the orange juice and process until combined.

Add the strawberries and banana and process until smooth.

Pour the mixture into tall glasses and decorate with slices of orange and whole strawberries.

Add straws and serve.

orange &
strawberry cream

black
& blue

Cultivated blackberries are consistently *plump and juicy*,

unlike their **hedgerow cousins**, which can be substituted if you have **a good supply**.

SERVES 2

generous ¾ cup cultivated **blackberries**

scant 1 cup blueberries

scant ½ **cup ice-cold water**

⅔ **cup plain yogurt**

Put the blackberries, blueberries, water, and yogurt into a food processor and process until smooth.

Pour into glasses and serve.

Serve this
in *tall thin glasses*
to **make the most** of its layers.

Mix the sugar and bread crumbs together and spread the mixture out on a baking sheet. Place under a moderate broiler or in a hot oven (400°F/200°C) for 7–10 minutes. Watch the crumbs carefully and turn frequently until they are nicely browned. Add the cinnamon and mix well. Let cool.

Pour boiling water over the peaches to scald them. Drain, then peel and cut into fourths, discarding the pits. Put into a food processor and process until smooth. Set aside and wash the food processor bowl. Put the milk and ice cream into the food processor and blend until combined.

Pour a little of the milk and ice cream mixture into each glass, then spoon over some peach purée and sprinkle over a few cinnamon bread crumbs. Carefully repeat these layers until you reach the top of the glass. Serve at once.

SERVES 2

2 tbsp soft dark brown sugar

2 tbsp soft brown bread crumbs

1 tsp ground cinnamon

4 ripe peaches

$^2/_3$ cup milk

3 large scoops of luxury vanilla ice cream

DECORATION

sugar and bread crumbs

peach &
cinnamon layer

fig &
maple melter

Go on,
indulge yourself

with this **rich, delicious, and sophisticated** smoothie.

SERVES 2

1½ **cups hazelnut yogurt**

2 **tbsp freshly squeezed orange juice**

4 **tbsp maple syrup**

8 **large fresh figs, chopped**

6 **ice cubes, crushed**

DECORATION

toasted chopped hazelnuts

Pour the yogurt, orange juice, and maple syrup into a food processor and process gently until combined.

Add the figs and ice cubes and process until smooth.

Pour the mixture into glasses and scatter over some toasted chopped hazelnuts.

Serve at once.

The *distinctive flavor* of fragrant, *ripe* apples

combines with fresh strawberries and freshly squeezed orange juice to give you a really zingy smoothie.

Put the apples, strawberries, and orange juice into a food processor and process until smooth.

Taste and sweeten with sugar if necessary.

Serve at once.

SERVES 2

2 ripe apples, peeled and coarsely chopped

generous $\frac{1}{3}$ cup strawberries, hulled

juice of 4 oranges

sugar, to taste

apple
cooler

peach &
red currant sunset

Make sure

the *peaches* you use

are **properly ripe** so their flavor counteracts the acidity of the red currants. This classic combination of flavors makes a **very pretty smoothie**. Run the prongs of a fork along each red currant stem to **release the red currants**.

SERVES 2

2 large ripe peaches

generous $^2/_3$ cup red currants

$^3/_4$ **cup ice-cold water**

1–2 tbsp clear honey

Halve the peaches and discard the pits. Coarsely chop the peaches and put into the food processor.

Keep 2 stems of red currants whole for decoration and strip the rest off their stems into a food processor. Add the water and honey and process until smooth.

Pour into glasses and decorate with the remaining red currant sprigs.

The *natural texture*
of the *honeydew* melon

lends itself to this delicate smoothie. For best results, make sure the melon is **truly ripe**.

Cut the rind off the melon. Chop the melon into chunks, discarding any seeds.

Put into a food processor with the water and honey and process until smooth.

Pour into glasses and decorate with a slice of strawberry or a cluster of red currants to set off the pale yellow.

SERVES 2

9 oz/250 g honeydew melon

1¼ cups sparkling mineral water

2 tbsp clear honey

DECORATION

red currant clusters

honeydew

juices, slushes, and floats

provide an instant supply of nutritional goodness: their life-giving benefits go straight into the body. The recipes in this chapter offer some exciting ideas, and after you have tried them, why not go on to experiment with your own combinations? The slushes included here are great revivers. They are especially refreshing on hot summer days.

Wake up *sweetie*,

or even ugli, depending on how you feel. **Sweetie grapefruit** and ugli fruit are very similar—a hybrid of grapefruit, they are **sweeter** and juicier, **perfect** to wake you up in the morning.

SERVES 2

Halve and squeeze the fruit into two glasses.

Add water and honey if liked.

Serve with a slice or two of lime or kiwi, floated on the surface and topped with a spoon of yogurt.

3 large ripe sweetie grapefruit or ugli fruit

$^2/_3$ cup sparkling water

1 tbsp flowery runny honey (optional)

some slices of lime or peeled kiwifruit

2 tbsp lowfat yogurt

wake up
sweetie

tomato

blazer

Tangy
and a *little bit hot*,

this is a juice with
a bit of **get-up-and-go**!

SERVES 2

generous 2 cups tomato juice

dash of Worcestershire sauce

**1 small red chile, deseeded
and chopped**

**1 scallion, trimmed
and chopped**

6 ice cubes, crushed

DECORATION

**2 long, thin red chiles,
cut into flowers**

To make the chile flowers, use a sharp knife to make six cuts along each chile. Place the point of the knife about ½ inch/1 cm from the stem end and cut toward the tip. Put the chiles in a bowl of iced water and let stand for 25–30 minutes, or until they have spread out into flower shapes.

Put the tomato juice and Worcestershire sauce into a food processor and process gently until combined. Add the chopped chile, scallion, and ice cubes and process until smooth.

Pour the mixture into glasses and garnish with the chile flowers.

Add straws and serve.

Use *large dark grapes*

for this foamy, refreshing cooler.

Put the grapes, mineral water, and lemon sherbet in a food processor and process until smooth.

Pour into glasses and serve immediately.

SERVES 2

scant 1 cup black grapes, deseeded or seedless

generous ¾ cup sparkling mineral water

2 large scoops of lemon sherbet

black grape

fizz

vegetable
cocktail

This *savory cocktail* combines all *the goodness*

of fresh vegetables in one glass.

SERVES 2

$^1/_2$ **cup carrot juice**

1 lb 2 oz/500 g tomatoes, skinned, deseeded, and coarsely chopped

1 tbsp lemon juice

4 celery stalks, trimmed and sliced

4 scallions, trimmed and coarsely chopped

scant $^1/_3$ cup fresh parsley

scant $^1/_3$ cup fresh mint

DECORATION

2 celery stalks

Put the carrot juice, tomatoes, and lemon juice into a food processor and process gently until combined.

Add the sliced celery along with the scallions, parsley, and mint and process until smooth.

Pour the mixture into glasses and garnish with celery stalks.

Serve at once.

Fresh, *clean*, and *simple*,

this is an **excellent** drink to serve on a **really hot day**. Loganberries are a delicious alternative to **raspberries** if you can find them.

Put the raspberries and water into a food processor and process until smooth.

Add the sherbet and process briefly until combined with the raspberry mixture.

Pour into glasses and drink while still slushy.

SERVES 2

½ **cup frozen raspberries**

1¼ **cups sparkling mineral water**

2 **scoops of black currant sherbet**

Raspberry

& black currant slush

carrot &
ginger energizer

This *stimulating* blend of flavors

is guaranteed to give you **a boost** when you need it.

SERVES **2**

1 cup carrot juice

4 tomatoes, skinned, deseeded, and coarsely chopped

1 tbsp lemon juice

scant ⅓ cup fresh parsley

1 tbsp grated fresh gingerroot

6 ice cubes, crushed

½ cup water

DECORATION

chopped fresh parsley

Put the carrot juice, tomatoes, and lemon juice into a food processor and process gently until combined.

Add the parsley to the food processor along with the ginger and ice cubes. Process until well combined, then pour in the water and process until smooth.

Pour the mixture into tall glasses and garnish with chopped fresh parsley.

Serve at once.

Now that *blood* (ruby) *orange juice*

is available all year round, you can use its **fabulous color** and **flavor** whenever you want.

Put the blood orange juice, strawberries, raspberries, and mineral water into a food processor and process until smooth. Strain the mixture to remove the seeds, if preferred.

Pour into glasses and serve.

SERVES 2

1 cup blood (ruby) orange juice

$2/3$ cup strawberries

$2/3$ cup raspberries

scant $1/4$ cup sparkling mineral water

blood orange *sparkler*

Grenadillos are members of the *passion fruit family.*

They are **very fragrant,** with a leathery orange skin hiding the **pulp and seeds.**

SERVES 2

3 ripe grenadillos

1 cup traditional sparkling lemonade

2 large scoops of mango sherbet

2 tsp grenadine syrup

Halve the grenadillos and scrape out the pulp and seeds into a strainer. Work the pulp through the strainer into a pitcher below.

Mix in the lemonade and pour into glasses.

Top with a scoop of mango sherbet and a teaspoon of grenadine syrup.

Serve.

grenadillo
float

carrot &
red bell pepper booster

This *dynamic* combination of *flavors* will fire up your system and boost your energy levels.

1 cup carrot juice

1 cup tomato juice

2 large red bell peppers, deseeded and coarsely chopped

1 tbsp lemon juice

freshly ground black pepper

Pour the carrot juice and tomato juice into a food processor and process gently until combined.

Add the red bell peppers and lemon juice. Season with plenty of freshly ground black pepper and process until smooth.

Pour the mixture into tall glasses, then add straws and serve.

strawberry &
pineapple refresher

Long-life *pineapple juice* and *frozen fruit*

are used in this easy-to-assemble **pantry smoothie**—the flavors are not compromised by your haste!

SERVES 2

1 cup frozen strawberries

1¼ cups long-life pineapple juice

1 tbsp superfine sugar

Put the strawberries, pineapple juice, and superfine sugar into a food processor and blend until smooth.

Serve at once.

This *medley* of *summer berries* makes an inspired drink.

Pour the orange juice, lime juice, and sparkling water into a food processor and process gently until combined.

Add the summer fruits and ice cubes and process until a slushy consistency has been reached.

Pour the mixture into glasses, then decorate with whole raspberries and blackberries on toothpicks and serve.

SERVES 2

4 tbsp orange juice

1 tbsp lime juice

scant $\frac{1}{2}$ cup sparkling water

$2\frac{1}{3}$ cups frozen summer fruits (such as blueberries, raspberries, blackberries, and strawberries)

4 ice cubes

DECORATION

fresh whole raspberries and blackberries on a toothpick

summer fruit
slush

homemade
lemonade

This *classic* cooler

is a well-loved, traditional favorite.

SERVES 2

²/₃ cup water

6 tbsp sugar

1 tsp grated lemon rind

¹/₂ cup lemon juice

6 ice cubes

TO SERVE

sparkling water

DECORATION

granulated sugar

slices of lemon

Put the water, sugar, and grated lemon rind into a small pan and bring to a boil, stirring constantly. Continue to boil, stirring, for 5 minutes.

Remove from the heat and let cool to room temperature. Stir in the lemon juice, then transfer to a pitcher and cover with plastic wrap. Chill in the refrigerator for at least 2 hours.

When the lemonade has almost finished chilling, take two glasses and rub the rims with a wedge of lemon, then dip them in granulated sugar to frost. Put the ice cubes into the glasses.

Remove the lemon syrup from the refrigerator, then pour it over the ice and top up with sparkling water. The ratio should be one part lemon syrup to three parts sparkling water. Stir well to mix. Decorate with sugar and slices of fresh lemon and serve.

Coffee and
a hint of *peppermint*

combine in this **delicious crush,**
which is topped by chocolate.

Pour the milk, coffee syrup, and peppermint
syrup into a food processor and process
gently until combined.

Add the mint and ice cubes and process until
a slushy consistency has been reached.

Pour the mixture into glasses. Scatter over
the grated chocolate, then decorate with
sprigs of fresh mint and serve.

SERVES 2

$1^{3}/_{4}$ **cups milk**

generous $^{3}/_{4}$ **cup coffee syrup**

scant $^{1}/_{2}$ **cup peppermint syrup**

1 tbsp chopped fresh mint leaves

4 ice cubes, crushed

DECORATION

grated chocolate

sprigs of fresh mint

iced coffee
& chocolate crush

christmas
in summer

This *looks* very *Christmassy*

with its **snowy top** suspended above the spiced ruby red liquid, but it is very **thirst-quenching** and works well as a summer cooler.

SERVES 2

generous ¼ cup cranberry cordial

2 allspice berries, crushed

2 slices of orange

2 cinnamon sticks

1 cup boiling water

2 scoops of luxury vanilla ice cream

Divide the cranberry cordial between 2 heatproof glasses, then add a crushed allspice berry, an orange slice, and a cinnamon stick to each glass.

With care, pour the boiling water into the glasses. Let cool, then chill.

When you are ready to serve, float a scoop of ice cream on the top of each glass.

When you
are *feeling jaded*,

this glorious pairing of **sweet** and **tart** flavors will perk you up and **give you a boost**.

Pour the pineapple juice and orange juice into a food processor and process gently until combined.

Add the melon, pineapple chunks, and ice cubes and process until a slushy consistency has been reached.

Pour the mixture into glasses and decorate with slices of melon and orange.

Serve at once.

SERVES 2

scant $\frac{1}{2}$ **cup pineapple juice**

4 **tbsp orange juice**

$4\frac{1}{2}$ **oz/125 g galia melon, cut into chunks**

1 **cup frozen pineapple chunks**

4 **ice cubes, crushed**

DECORATION

slices of galia melon

slices of orange

melon &
pineapple crush

milk shakes have never

lost their popularity. In fact, they seem to be more popular than ever. Milk shakes come in a wide variety of flavors and can be thick or not so thick, depending on the ratio of solid ingredients to milk. For example, many of them contain ice cream, and you can experiment with the thickness by varying the ratio of ice cream to liquid. You can also ring the changes by using a different flavor of ice cream, or by substituting one type of fruit for another.

spiced
banana
milk shake

This is a *Caribbean* combination of *fruit* and *spices* that will tantalize the tastebuds.

SERVES 2

1¼ **cups milk**

½ **tsp allspice**

5½ **oz/150 g banana ice cream**

2 bananas, sliced and frozen

Pour the milk into a food processor and add the allspice. Add half of the banana ice cream and process gently until combined, then add the remaining ice cream and process until well blended.

When the mixture is well combined, add the bananas and process until smooth.

Pour the mixture into tall glasses. Add straws and serve at once.

You will need

perfectly ripe plums

for this **fabulously frothy**, fruity recipe. Dark ones—such as Marjorie's Seedling—give a **better color**.

Put the plums, milk, and ice cream into a food processor and process until smooth and frothy.

Pour into glasses and serve at once with crumbly oat cookies.

SERVES 2

4 medium ripe plums, pitted

generous ¾ cup ice-cold milk

2 scoops of luxury vanilla ice cream

TO SERVE

crumbly oat cookies

plum
fluff

peach

bliss

Different *fruits* combine with *peaches*

to make one **marvelously fruity** drink.

SERVES 2

¾ **cup milk**

1 cup canned peach slices, drained

2 fresh apricots, chopped

2²/₃ cups fresh strawberries, hulled and sliced

2 bananas, sliced and frozen

DECORATION
slice of strawberry

Pour the milk into a food processor. Add the peach slices and process gently until combined. Add the apricots and process gently until combined.

Add the strawberries and banana slices and process until smooth.

Pour the mixture into glasses and decorate the rims with fresh strawberries.

Serve at once.

Mango and *nectarine*
is an inspired combination
of fruits, made **all the more special** with the clever addition of lemon sherbet.

Pour the milk into a food processor, then add half of the lemon sherbet and process gently until combined. Add the remaining sherbet and process until smooth.

When the mixture is thoroughly blended, gradually add the mango and nectarines and process until smooth.

Pour the mixture into glasses, then add straws and serve.

1 cup milk

12 oz/350 g lemon sherbet

1 ripe mango, pitted and diced

2 ripe nectarines, pitted and diced

smooth
nectarine shake

tropical
storm

Revive *yourself*

with this **invigorating** and **exuberant** tropical shake.

SERVES **2**

1 cup milk

scant $\frac{1}{2}$ cup coconut milk

$5\frac{1}{2}$ oz/150 g vanilla ice cream

2 bananas, sliced and frozen

scant $1\frac{1}{2}$ cups canned pineapple chunks, drained

1 papaya, deseeded and diced

DECORATION

grated fresh coconut

wedges of fresh pineapple

Pour the milk and coconut milk into a food processor and process gently until combined. Add half of the ice cream and process gently, then add the remaining ice cream and process until smooth.

Add the bananas and process well, then add the pineapple chunks and papaya and process until smooth.

Pour the mixture into tall glasses. Scatter the grated coconut over the shakes and decorate the rims with pineapple wedges.

Serve at once.

The *ultimate*
strawberry milk shake!

Forget about **synthetic** strawberry-flavored syrups—this is the real thing: a gorgeous flavor and **fantastically** fruity. Set off the pale coloring with some pretty **green mint leaves**.

Put the strawberries, cream, milk, and superfine sugar into a food processor and process until smooth.

Pour into glasses and serve decorated with mint leaves.

SERVES 2

1 cup frozen strawberries

scant $\frac{1}{2}$ cup light cream

generous $\frac{3}{4}$ cup cold whole milk

1 tbsp superfine sugar

DECORATION

mint leaves

strawberries
& cream milk shake

Perfect Plum
shake

A *deep*, *rich*,

and *fruity* shake

for the **end of the summer**.

SERVES 2

9 oz/250 g plums

generous ¾ cup water

1 tbsp golden granulated sugar

4 scoops of frozen yogurt (plain)
or ice cream

2 Italian almond or
pistachio biscotti, crumbled

TO SERVE

extra biscotti, crumbled

Put the plums, water, and sugar into a small pan. Cover tightly and simmer for about 15 minutes, or until the plums have split and are very soft. Let cool.

Strain off the liquid into a food processor and add the frozen yogurt or ice cream. Process until smooth and frothy.

Pour into glasses and sprinkle with the crumbled biscotti. Serve with extra biscotti on the side.

A *powerhouse*

for those who lead **an active life—
this milk shake** tastes fabulous, too.

Pour the milk into a food processor, then add the coffee powder and process gently until combined. Add half of the vanilla ice cream and process gently, then add the remaining ice cream and process until well combined.

When the mixture is thoroughly blended, add the bananas and process until smooth.

Pour the mixture into glasses and serve.

SERVES 2

1¼ **cups milk**

4 **tbsp instant coffee powder**

5½ **oz/150 g vanilla ice cream**

2 **bananas, sliced and frozen**

coffee banana
cooler

raspberry
ripple rice cream

A fresh-tasting, *nondairy shake* with *no* animal products,

no cholesterol, no lactose, and no problem! Rice "milk" should be **kept cold** in the refrigerator for the **best-tasting results**. Soy milk can be used instead, but the rice "milk" tastes much nicer.

SERVES 2

generous ¾ cup frozen raspberries

1¼ cups rice "milk"

or soy milk

Put the raspberries and half the rice "milk" into a food processor and process until smooth.

Strain into a pitcher and carefully stir through the remaining rice "milk" to give a marbled effect.

Pour into glasses and serve still very cold.

A *luscious* combination of fruits

to leave you **restored, revived,** and **refreshed**.

Pour the milk, yogurt, and orange juice into a food processor and process gently until combined.

Add the peach slices and ice cubes and process until smooth. Pour the mixture into glasses and decorate with strips of orange peel.

Add straws and serve.

SERVES 2

scant ½ cup milk

½ cup peach yogurt

scant ½ cup orange juice

1 cup canned peach slices, drained

6 ice cubes, crushed

DECORATION

strips of orange peel

peach &
orange milk shake

buttermilk shake

Although it tastes *deliciously rich*,

cultured buttermilk is **low in fat** and makes a **lovely creamy** milk shake. The buttermilk is combined with **strawberries** here, but you can substitute any other soft fruit.

SERVES 2

generous ³/₄ **cup frozen**
strawberries
1¹/₄ **cups cultured buttermilk**
¹/₂ **tsp vanilla extract**
2 **tbsp superfine sugar**

DECORATION

slices of strawberry

Put the strawberries, buttermilk, vanilla extract, and superfine sugar into a food processor and process until smooth.

Decorate the rims of the glasses with strawberry slices. Serve at once, with straws.

The ultimate
milk shake

for **children** and **chocoholics** alike, this drink is **supremely satisfying**.

Pour the milk and chocolate syrup into a food processor and process gently until combined.

Add the chocolate ice cream and process until smooth. Pour the mixture into tall glasses and scatter the grated chocolate over the shakes.

Serve at once.

SERVES 2

$^2/_3$ **cup milk**

2 tbsp chocolate syrup

14 oz/400 g chocolate ice cream

DECORATION

grated chocolate

chocolate *milk shake*

banana

breakfast shake

Milk and *honey* team up with *bananas*

for a **dreamy shake** that is the perfect **start to the day**.

SERVES 2

2 ripe bananas

³/₄ cup/2 tbsp sour cream

¹/₂ **cup milk**

2 tbsp clear honey, plus extra for drizzling

¹/₂ tsp vanilla extract

Put the bananas, sour cream, milk, honey, and vanilla extract into a food processor and process until smooth.

Serve at once, drizzled with a little more honey on top.

Maple, vanilla, and *almond*

are **delicate flavors** that **complement** each other perfectly.

Pour the milk and maple syrup into a food processor and process gently until combined.

Add the ice cream and almond extract and process until smooth.

Pour the mixture into glasses and scatter the chopped nuts over the shakes.

Add straws and serve.

SERVES 2

²/₃ **cup milk**

2 tbsp maple syrup

14 oz/400 g vanilla ice cream

1 tbsp almond extract

DECORATION

chopped almonds

creamy
maple shake

guava
goodness

Guavas are remarkably high in *vitamin C*,

and, when blended with milk, provide a very **nutritious start** to any day.

SERVES 2

14 oz/400 g canned guavas, drained

1 cup ice-cold milk

TO SERVE

cereal bars (optional)

Place the guavas into a food processor and pour in the milk. Process until well blended.

Strain into glasses to remove the hard seeds. Serve with a cereal bar if liked.

Surprisingly
both hot and cold

on the tongue, this **minty cooler** will **restore vitality** and vigor.

Pour the milk and peppermint syrup into a food processor and process gently until combined.

Add the peppermint ice cream and process until smooth.

Pour the mixture into tall glasses and decorate with sprigs of fresh mint.

Add straws and serve.

SERVES 2

$^2/_3$ **cup milk**

2 tbsp peppermint syrup

14 oz/400 g peppermint ice cream

DECORATION

sprigs of fresh mint

peppermint
refresher

apricot &
almond milk

Almond milk is used around the *Mediterranean*

and is **best made** with new season's nuts. It is fiddly to blanch and peel almonds, but the **extra flavor** is worth it. You can use ready-blanched nuts but not **ground or slivered almonds**.

SERVES 2

generous 1 cup fresh almonds

1¼ cups boiling water, plus water for scalding

4 ripe apricots

2 tsp raw sugar

Pour some boiling water over the almonds to scald them. Drain them and, as soon as the nuts are cool enough to handle, slip off the brown skins and put the kernels into the food processor with ⅔ cup boiling water. Grind the nuts and water in the food processor, then add another ⅔ cup water and process again. Strain and let cool. Rinse out the food processor.

Pour boiling water over the apricots to scald them. Drain, then peel and cut into fourths, discarding the pits. Put them in the food processor and purée. Combine the almond milk and the apricot purée in the food processor and process until blended.

Pour into glasses and top with a crunchy layer of raw sugar.

This *drink* provides *a good source*

of vitamin C, as well as a wonderfully refreshing sweet and sharp flavor.

Pour the milk and lime juice into a food processor and process gently until combined.

Add the kiwifruit and sugar and process gently, then add the ice cream and process until smooth.

Pour the mixture into glasses and decorate with slices of kiwifruit and strips of lime peel.

Serve at once.

SERVES 2

$^2/_3$ cup milk

juice of 2 limes

2 kiwifruit, chopped

1 tbsp sugar

14 oz/400 g vanilla ice cream

DECORATION

slices of kiwifruit

strips of lime peel

kiwi
& lime shake

drinks for entertaining

include a mouthwatering array of ingredients and flavors, from the stunning Mocha Cream— a feast of coffee, cream, and chocolate—to the delicately perfumed Lassi. These drinks will tantalize every palate. Yet the good news is that all are, or can be, alcohol-free, so everyone can enjoy them. You can make them as decorative as you like: suggestions for decoration have been given here, but feel free to experiment with your own.

mocha

cream

The *heavenly* pairing
of coffee and chocolate

can **be improved only** by
the addition of **whipped cream**.

SERVES 2

generous ³/₄ **cup milk**

scant ¹/₄ **cup light cream**

1 tbsp brown sugar

2 tbsp unsweetened cocoa

**1 tbsp coffee syrup or instant
coffee powder**

6 ice cubes

DECORATION

whipped cream

grated chocolate

Put the milk, cream, and sugar into a
food processor and process gently until
combined.

Add the unsweetened cocoa and coffee
syrup or powder and process well, then add
the ice cubes and process until smooth.

Pour the mixture into glasses. Top with
whipped cream, then scatter the grated
chocolate over the drinks and serve.

This is a *twist* on a *classic cocktail.*

Make sure the **champagne** or Moscato di Spumante is thoroughly chilled **before you begin**.

Pour boiling water over the peaches to scald them. Drain, then peel and chop them, discarding the pits.

Put the chopped peaches into a food processor and process until smooth.

Divide the peach mixture between 2 champagne flutes. Stir in the champagne or sparkling wine, mixing with a swizzle stick.

Serve at once with a few amaretti cookies.

SERVES 2

2 large ripe peaches

1¼ cups chilled demi-sec champagne, Moscato di Spumante, or other sparkling white wine

(for a nonalcoholic version use sparkling grape juice)

TO SERVE

amaretti cookies

bellini

iced coffee
with cream

After a lazy *alfresco* lunch,

what could be nicer than this **cool**, **sophisticated** iced coffee?

SERVES 2

1³/₄ **cups water**

2 tbsp instant coffee granules

2 tbsp brown sugar

6 ice cubes, crushed

DECORATION

light cream

whole coffee beans

Use the water and coffee granules to brew some hot coffee, then let cool to room temperature. Transfer to a pitcher, then cover with plastic wrap and chill in the refrigerator for at least 45 minutes.

When the coffee has chilled, pour it into a food processor. Add the sugar and process until well combined. Add the ice cubes and process until smooth.

Pour the mixture into glasses. Float light cream on the top, then decorate with whole coffee beans and serve.

The famous *Italian* pudding

brought to you in a glass is the most delicious luxury.

SERVES 2

Pour the espresso into 2 glasses and mix with the granulated sugar and Amaretto.

Blend the mascarpone, egg yolk or milk, vanilla extract, and superfine sugar until smooth.

Hold the back of a warm dry teaspoon just above the coffee in the glasses and pour the mascarpone mixture into the glasses over it so it floats on top of the coffee.

Dust with unsweetened cocoa or crushed chocolate flake.

Serve with ladyfingers for dipping.

Note: this recipe contains raw eggs, so should be avoided by infants, the elderly, pregnant women, convalescents, and anyone suffering from an illness.

generous ¾ cup freshly made espresso coffee

1 tbsp golden granulated sugar

1 tbsp Amaretto liqueur or Marsala

4 tbsp mascarpone cheese

1 egg yolk or 1 tbsp milk

½ tsp vanilla extract

1 tbsp superfine sugar

1 tsp unsweetened cocoa or a little crushed chocolate flake

TO SERVE

ladyfingers

tiramisù
treat

coffee
hazelnut soda

Add a *little soda sparkle*

to your life—you will be **pleasantly surprised** by how well this mix works.

SERVES 2

1 cup water

3 tbsp instant coffee granules

1/2 cup sparkling water

1 tbsp hazelnut syrup

2 tbsp brown sugar

6 ice cubes, crushed

DECORATION

slices of lime

slices of lemon

Use the water and coffee granules to brew some hot coffee, then let cool to room temperature.

Transfer to a pitcher, then cover with plastic wrap and chill in the refrigerator for at least 45 minutes.

When the coffee has chilled, pour it into a food processor. Add the sparkling water, hazelnut syrup, and sugar, and process well. Add the ice cubes and process until smooth.

Pour the mixture into glasses. Decorate the rims with slices of fresh lime and lemon, and serve.

spiced *lemon tea*

An *aromatic* *warm* drink,

which is perfect at any time of year.

SERVES 2

1³/₄ cups water

4 cloves

1 small stick of cinnamon

2 tea bags

3–4 tbsp lemon juice

1–2 tbsp brown sugar

DECORATION

slices of lemon

Put the water, cloves, and cinnamon into a pan and bring to a boil. Remove from the heat and add the tea bags. Let infuse for 5 minutes, then remove the tea bags.

Stir in lemon juice and sugar to taste. Return the pan to the heat and warm through gently.

Remove the pan from the heat and strain the tea into heatproof glasses. Decorate with slices of lemon and serve.

Chocolate and *cherries*

are a classic combination.

You can also serve this **white chocolate and black cherry smoothie** as a dessert, with a couple of **dark chocolate thins**.

SERVES 2

Halve and pit the black cherries. Put these into a food processor and process until puréed.

Add the ice cream and milk and process briefly to mix well.

Pour into glasses, adding long-handled soda spoons.

$^3/_4$ **cup black cherries**

3 large scoops of luxury white chocolate ice cream

$^2/_3$ **cup milk**

black
& white
smoothie

lassi

Traditionally served as *an accompaniment*

to a hot Indian curry, **lassi** makes the **perfect cooler**.

SERVES 2

scant ½ cup plain yogurt

generous 2 cups milk

1 tbsp rose water

3 tbsp honey

1 ripe mango, pitted and diced

6 ice cubes

DECORATION

edible rose petals, optional

Pour the yogurt and milk into a food processor and process gently until combined.

Add the rose water and honey and process until thoroughly blended, then add the mango along with the ice cubes and process until smooth.

Pour the mixture into glasses. Decorate with edible rose petals, if using, and serve.

Cherry soda looks very *elegant* and it tastes **perfect**, too.

Divide the crushed ice between two glasses. Pour the cherry syrup over the ice.

Top up each glass with sparkling water. Decorate with the maraschino cherries on toothpicks and serve.

SERVES 2

8 ice cubes, crushed

2 tbsp cherry syrup

generous 2 cups sparkling water

DECORATION

maraschino cherries
on a toothpick

cherry
soda

iced
citrus tea

the *combination* of sweet and sharp

citrus flavors turns this into an irresistible drink.

SERVES 2

1¼ cups water

2 tea bags

scant ½ cup orange juice

4 tbsp lime juice

1–2 tbsp brown sugar

8 ice cubes

DECORATION

wedge of lime

granulated sugar

slices of orange, lemon, or lime

Pour the water into a pan and bring to a boil. Remove from the heat, then add the tea bags and let infuse for 5 minutes. Remove the tea bags and then let the tea cool to room temperature (about 30 minutes). Transfer to a pitcher, then cover with plastic wrap and chill in the refrigerator for at least 45 minutes.

When the tea has chilled, pour in the orange juice and lime juice. Add sugar to taste.

Take two glasses and rub the rims with a wedge of lime, then dip them in granulated sugar to frost. Put the ice cubes into the glasses and pour over the tea. Decorate the rims with slices of fresh orange, lemon, or lime and serve.

Set off the *beautiful green color* of this smoothie

by placing a **strawberry or two** on **the rim of the glass**.

Put the kiwifruit, melon balls, lemon sherbet, and water into a food processor and process until smooth.

Pour into glasses and serve.

SERVES 2

2 ripe kiwifruit,
peeled and cut into fourths

7 oz/200 g frozen Galia melon balls

2 scoops lemon sherbet

2 tbsp water

DECORATION

strawberries

green
gala

Shirley
Temple

A classic nonalcoholic cocktail

with movie star **appeal**.

SERVES 2

SUGAR SYRUP **8 tbsp water** **8 tbsp superfine sugar**	Make the sugar syrup by dissolving the sugar in the water over low heat. Bring to a boil, then continue to boil without stirring for 1–2 minutes.
20 cracked ice cubes **scant ½ cup lemon juice** **1 tbsp grenadine**	Put half the cracked ice cubes into a cocktail shaker. Pour the lemon juice, grenadine, and sugar syrup over the ice and shake vigorously.
ginger ale (to top up)	Half fill two small, chilled glasses with cracked ice cubes and strain the drink over them. Top up with ginger ale.
DECORATION **slice of orange** **cocktail cherry**	Decorate with a slice of orange and a cherry.

Don't try
to *squeeze the pomegranate*

in an **electric juicer,** or you will make the juice bitter. This is a lovely **late summer drink** made with the **new season's pomegranates,** which start to appear in stores in August.

SERVES 2

Cut the pomegranates in half and extract the juice with an old-fashioned lemon squeezer.

2 ripe pomegranates

Halve the passion fruit and strain the pulp into a small bowl. Mix in the pomegranate juice and honey.

1 passion fruit

1 tbsp clear honey

2 glasses full of crushed ice

Pour over the crushed ice and serve.

pomegranate
passion

raspberry
& apple quencher

Quick and *easy to make,*

this is a **simple and elegant** drink to enjoy.

SERVES 2

8 ice cubes, crushed

2 tbsp raspberry syrup

generous 2 cups chilled apple juice

Divide the crushed ice between two glasses and pour over the raspberry syrup.

Top up each glass with chilled apple juice and stir well.

DECORATION

whole raspberries and pieces of apple on toothpicks

Decorate with the whole raspberries and pieces of apple on toothpicks and serve.

While this drink
looks and tastes fabulous,

it has lots of **health-giving** carotene and vitamin C.

Pour the carrot juice and orange juice into a food processor and process gently until well combined. Add the ice cream and process until thoroughly blended.

Add the ice and process until smooth. Pour the mixture into glasses, then decorate with slices of orange and strips of orange peel and serve.

SERVES 2

$3/4$ **cup carrot juice**

$3/4$ **cup orange juice**

$5^1/_2$ **oz/150 g vanilla ice cream**

6 ice cubes, crushed

DECORATION

slices of orange

strips of orange peel

carrot
& orange cream

black currant
bracer